BOOK 8

ALL ABOUT
EVERGREENS

JOHN BRADSHAW'S
COMPLETE GUIDE TO
BETTER GARDENING
IN SIXTEEN VOLUMES

"Copyright Owners"

LELAND PUBLISHING COMPANY

NEW YORK • BUFFALO • TORONTO

Year of Publication 1961

©

Printed in U.S.A.

TABLE OF CONTENTS

Courtesy of A. B. Morse Co.

Evergreens add great beauty to any part of the garden

ALL ABOUT EVERGREENS

INTRODUCTION

The delicate tracery of twig and bough
Stands revealed against winter's frosty
sky.
Brings us the airs of hills and forest,
The sweet aroma of birch and pine;
Give us a waft of the north wind laden
With sweet brier odors and breath of
kine.

John Greenleaf Whittier

This is how one of the world's greatest poets felt about evergreens. Whether using them in the foundation planting, shrub border, as specimen trees, or as a hedge,

you not only add great beauty to the garden, but also bring to it much history and dignity.

Next time you see evergreens, pause for a moment and try to realize that their ancestors were on the earth ages before man, and indeed are the oldest living things on the earth.

Sequoias growing on the mountainsides in California were large specimens at the time Moses led the Children of Israel out of Egypt towards the Promised Land. Isaiah mentioned them in the 41st verse and 19th chapter of his book when he said "I will set in the desert a fir tree and a pine".

There are other evergreens in China that

Courtesy of A. B. Morse Co.

Evergreens bring dignity and history to the garden

The only greenery during the winter months is provided by evergreens

are much older than those in California. In Mexico, an evergreen known as the Cypress del Tule has survived thousands of years and is now so big it throws a ground shadow covering an area of 7,200 square feet. Legend has it that Cortez and his army were able to camp beneath it on a march to the Honduras.

There is no doubt that the first Christmas tree was one of the evergreens, and from this has grown the lovely custom we now enjoy so much at Christmas time.

Evergreens in the garden not only bring beauty and softness during the Summer season, but provide the only greenery during the Winter months when the flowers, shrubs and trees are dormant. It would be very hard to match the majesty of an evergreen silhouetted against a background of fleecy white snow.

We mentioned earlier that evergreens are the oldest forms of life on earth, when planted in the garden they bestow a gracious permanence not often found with other plant life. Given good care and soil conditions an evergreen will continue to flourish and give forth year-round beauty for your lifetime, that of the garden and for many years beyond.

Evergreens and their many uses in the garden

Although evergreens are widely planted in foundation beds surrounding the sides of houses, many people neglect to use them elsewhere in the garden. Tall, well-grown evergreens such as Koster blue spruce and Austrian pine planted as individual specimen trees at the back or the sides of the garden stand proud and erect presenting a picture of beauty.

Other tall growing kinds can be used to screen unsightly views or to provide an attractive and year-round background for the patio or outdoor living area.

In the colder parts, especially in the country, much more use could be made of evergreens as windbreaks, and as a real and effective form of climate control. It is a fact that evergreens or other trees, placed so they shade the west side of the house, will lower the roof and wall temperatures in the Summer as much as 20 to 40 degrees. In the Winter, the evergreens act as a windbreak, and make really substantial savings in fuel costs. For instance, it takes twice as much fuel to heat a house when it is 32 degrees outside with a 12 miles an hour wind blow-

Evergreens give a permanence not provided by any other plant life

Courtesy of A. B. Morse Co.

Courtesy of A. B. Morse Co.

It's much better to provide a permanent foundation bed rather than setting evergreens in lawn as pictured

ing, as it does when the wind is blowing at 3 miles an hour.

Evergreens are ideal for using in all types of landscaping because they are so persistent, lasting from season to season and year to year. It is really surprising the variety of colors they offer at different seasons. They are also desirable because they do not grow quickly out of bounds.

There are several evergreens which will grow well when planted in the shade. For

planting locations on the north side of the house, or in any spot which is quite shady, it is advisable to plant the yews or hemlocks. The spreading and low-growing evergreen known as Pfitzer's juniper or the dwarf and compact Mugho pine are admirably suited to partial shade conditions.

Many persons wish to plant evergreens on cemetery plots, and this is a wise choice on their part. They lend a unique touch of color to the dull and bleak Winter land-

Courtesy of A. B. Morse Co.

Evergreens come in a variety of colors to brighten the winter scene

scape, and add much overall beauty during Spring, Summer and Fall. However, before buying and planting any evergreens for this purpose, be sure to find out what cemetery regulations exist regarding private plantings. Many cemeteries regulate such plantings to avoid disturbing the master landscape plan of the cemetery. You will usually discover that the officials in charge are only too happy to help you choose the right evergreens for the purpose you have in mind and to give you expert advice on their planting and maintenance. One of the best evergreens for cemetery use is the Japanese yew, with its rich, deep green color, and its ability to withstand considerable shade.

Evergreens to brighten the Winter scene

Ask the average person to state the color

The golden juniper Pfitzer's Aurea

Courtesy of McConnell Nurseries, Port Burwell, Ont.

of evergreens, and he would immediately answer, "Green, of course". This answer would be only partially right, for while most evergreens are green in color, the needle bearing types grow in a wide variety of colors, including blue, silver, gold and lavender. When other trees are bare of leaves from the end of October to the middle of May, the evergreen takes over the coloring of the winter scene in the garden.

PLANTING AND CARE OF EVERGREENS

Plan before you buy—Planting evergreens requires a lot of thought and planning, the trees and shrubs must be planted for permanence, and so must be correctly placed at the start.

You must first decide on the type of evergreens suitable for your purpose. Find out the trees and shrubs best suited for your locality, the mature height and width of trees and the area covered by the spreading varieties at maturity. Armed with this knowledge you will soon arrive at the conclusion that in front of the average house, there is only sufficient space for six ever-

Ageratum and other low growing flowers can be planted at the front of the foundation bed for added beauty

Courtesy of A. B. Morse Co.

greens at the most. At first, this will mean there will be a number of bare spaces and large parts of the foundation wall will be visible. Have no misgivings about this as the spaces can be filled with good effect by planting annuals, bulbs, shrubs, biennials and perennials. The flowers will add color and charm to the new foundation planting.

Resist the temptation to fill the spaces with further evergreens. Over-planting evergreens, particularly in foundation plantings

is probably the biggest single mistake made in gardening by beginners. Immediately evergreens are planted they produce a very pleasing effect, it is this effect which compels some people to buy more than is necessary.

Over-planting and the incorrect setting of evergreens can produce unpleasant effects, some bordering as nuisance. For instance, a beautiful Blue spruce bought when 3 feet high can grow to 90 feet at maturity. Badly

Overplanting and incorrect setting of evergreens can produce unpleasant effects

Courtesy of A. B. Mörse Co.

placed, it will obstruct the view or may foul hydro wires. Over-planted foundation plantings are monotonous and so do not display the evergreens at their best advantage.

The removal of trees can be very expensive, especially as mechanical equipment will have to be used in most cases. In many gardens, it would be difficult to move the equipment into place without some other damage to the garden.

With the exception of some species of yew, evergreens should not be pruned repressively. This is mentioned as some people may think they can successfully cut back an evergreen once it has grown too large. If you try to head back a Blue spruce, it will either die or develop a new center from one of the side limbs, thus causing the tree to grow in a grotesque shape.

Before employing a landscaping firm to set your foundation planting or other evergreens make sure you are dealing with a

The gold of the petite strain of marigolds effectively contrasts with the color of the evergreens

Courtesy of The Geo. J. Ball Inc., West Chicago, Ill.

Courtesy of A. B. Morse Co.

Here is a typical example of an evergreen planted too close to the house

thoroughly reliable company. Do not hesitate to call your local horticultural club or the Better Business Bureau as any unethical practises carried out will be costly in the long run.

For real satisfaction in obtaining evergreens, be absolutely sure as to your requirements and see you get the best value for your money.

Evergreens in the foundation planting

To be successful, foundation planting beds should be at least six feet wide. This is the absolute minimum, as eight to ten feet would be more appropriate. This may seem unduly wide, but the latter is within the scope of most gardens, and there are very sound reasons for the width.

Over-planting is one of the biggest mistakes made by both beginners to gardening and by unethical landscape men. It is certainly true there are more mistakes made in the foundation planting than in any other part of the garden.

Most foundation beds are far too small. Usually they consist of an oblong bed about three feet wide along the front and sides of the house. This lack of width is a very serious mistake because first of all we have to have enough room so that every evergreen can be located at least three feet from the foundation wall. Furthermore, the foundation planting has to be large enough to hold a representative selection of flowering shrubs, spring flowering bulbs, biennials such as violas and pansies, summer annuals and the odd perennial.

When the foundation bed is very narrow the evergreens are planted too close to the foundation wall. This can actually give an evergreen a "schizophrenic" personality in the Wintertime. The modern basement radiates heat through the foundation wall and when evergreens are planted only a foot or so from the wall, the root of the tree next to it senses that Spring has arrived. However the roots on the outside of the tree will be still in the grip of Winter. The root near the wall may start to grow during mild spells only to be damaged when the weather turns cold again. The heat also dries out the soil, and since evergreens continually give off moisture through their needles, even on days when the temperature falls to zero or lower, they can easily be in serious need of water in the midst of Winter.

There is another and still more important reason for not planting too close to the

Petunias like Pink Magic are fine for filling in the bare spots in the foundation planting

Courtesy of A. B. Morse Co.

Overplanting is a major fault in foundation beds

foundation wall. It may not be readily realized that during hot Summer days the sun's rays are reflected by house walls causing ground temperatures as high as 175 degrees one or two feet from the wall. This is only 37 degrees removed from the boiling point of water so it is no wonder that evergreens turn brown and die.

The man who has just bought a newly built house, or the person who is having trouble with evergreens, should examine the soil carefully where the foundation planting is either located or planned. All too often, when the builder or plasterer is finished with the house, any refuse left over indoors is pushed through the front doors or windows becoming mixed with the soil lying immediately in front of the house.

Building refuse almost invariably contains lime, and this is sure death to evergreens. Lime not only harms evergreens and other plants immediately after planting, but persists for a number of years.

Unless you are sure the soil around your house is good garden or farm soil, and it is free from lime and other debris, the best plan is to dig out the existing soil and replace it with a good top soil mixture. To ensure success, the existing soil should be removed to a depth of two feet. This may seem like a lot of work at the time, and it may be expensive, but in the long run it will pay off as it will save you disappointment, expense and labor over the succeeding years. Furthermore, the results will fully justify your efforts.

How to plant Evergreens — The best insurance for growing evergreens successfully is to have the soil in which they are planted composed of one third to one half humus. The top soil should not be black soil from woods or swamps, but good farm or garden top soil which can come either from your own garden or from one of the commercially prepared mixtures.

A great percentage of the evergreens sold in North America every year come from the Boskoop district of Holland where the evergreens thrive in a humus rich soil. Throughout this region the soil contains so much humus that when walking on it, one bounces as if on springs. For humus there is a wide choice of excellent materials, including materials processed from sewage, discarded mushroom manure, well-rotted barnyard manure, leaf mold, or material from the home compost heap.

The day you bring your evergreens home from the nursery or garden center is the day to plant them. However, if this is not practicable, it is possible to keep them for two or three days as long as they are kept in a shaded spot protected from the wind. Best plan is to set the tree in moist earth without removing the burlap making sure you spray or sprinkle the needles daily with water until you have the opportunity to plant them.

The planting operation for evergreens can be divided into five easy and simple steps.

1. You make a start by digging a planting

This is what can happen when too many evergreens are planted in the beginning

Courtesy of A. B. Morse Co.

The soil in which you plant evergreens must contain plenty of humus

hole several inches wider and deeper than is necessary to hold the burlapped ball of earth covering the roots. A planting hole two feet wide and two feet in depth is a good rule to follow as far as evergreens are concerned.

What do we mean by a burlapped ball of earth? When moving evergreens from the nursery to the garden, a ball of soil is kept around the roots to prevent the evergreen receiving too severe a shock and setback because of the moving. The burlap or similar material is used to hold the soil in place.

Many garden centers and nurseries now stock evergreens planted in soil, soluble pots or other containers which means they can be transplanted any time during Spring, Summer or Fall. Nurserymen expect that in

the future most evergreens sold will be treated this way. However, at the moment, many are being sold balled in the burlap and must be handled carefully at planting time to avoid separation of the soil from the roots.

2. When placing the tree in the planting hole, do not remove the burlap around the ball, as it will rot away a few weeks after planting. All you need to do is to loosen the burlap around the trunk and either roll it back or cut away the top with a sharp knife. The time to do this is after setting the evergreens in place in the planting hole.

3. Evergreens should be planted just a trifle lower in the ground than they stood at the nursery. If you examine the trunk of the tree closely, you will be able to see the soil

line as it existed in the nursery.

4. Fill in three or four inches of the special planting soil mixture and firm it well around the ball of earth to eliminate any air pockets. Then fill in another 3 or 4 inches of the mixture and firm as before. By this time the planting hole will be about half full of the soil mixture. Next, take the hose or the watering can and fill the remainder of the hole with water. This is done to further ensure the earth is well settled around the evergreen ball and that any possible air pockets are completely eliminated. Let the water drain completely away before filling in the remainder of the soil.

5. If you go for a walk in the woods and observe the conditions under which evergreens grow in nature you will discover that they always have a thick mulch of needles, leaves and other leafy plant materials covering the soil for a wide area from the trunk to well beyond the outer spread of the branches. This helps to keep the roots cool in summer and preserves the available. moisture in the soil.

Just as soon as you have finished planting is the time to duplicate this mulch in the garden or foundation planting. Spread a mulch of humus at least two to three inches deep and extending from the trunk to well beyond the spread of the branches. There is a wide choice of humus materials that can be used for the mulching of evergreens. All of them have equal merit as far as their value as mulches is concerned the deciding factor of which to use being the material

Plant evergreens a trifle lower than they stood at the nursery

Courtesy of A. B. Morse Co.

Courtesy of The Geo. J. Ball Inc., West Chicago, Ill.

Petunias and evergreens combine for a fine display

that looks the best in your garden.

Any of the following makes a good mulch for evergreens. Peat moss, materials processed from sewage, well-rotted barnyard manure, grass clippings, discarded mushroom manure, compost, leaf mold, and vermiculite materials.

Late in the Fall these can be dug into the soil to increase its supply of humus. The following Spring a fresh mulch can be put down.

Be sure to give the evergreens a good soaking right after planting, and keep up the watering right through the first Summer. This does not mean that you should water every day, for this is bad, not only for evergreens, but for any part of the garden. A good soaking once a week is the best plan.

You will be giving the evergreens a good soaking if the water penetrates to a depth of 7 or 8 inches.

Watering Evergreens—Evergreens in the home garden need to be watered regularly from May until freeze-up time.

You may contend that evergreens growing in the woods never receive any moisture except that by the rains. However, these evergreens have the advantage of having a deep, cool, moist mulch of humus extending a long way beyond the outer spread of the branches. This not only helps to preserve the moisture in the soil but also keeps the roots cool during the hot days of July and early August. We must also remember that evergreens in the woods have an extensive root system which can penetrate deeply to reach the permanent water table.

Compare these conditions with those in the average home garden. In the foundation planting they have a next-to-the-wall location where they suffer from the hot reflected rays of the sun during July and August, and are subject to the heat given off through basement walls from the furnace during the Winter.

In the garden there is usually no natural mulch to hold the moisture, and in all too many cases no other mulch is applied. The result is that when the weather turns hot, the ground dries out rapidly and easily. Under these conditions evergreens have to grow to a considerable size before their roots will go down deeply enough into the soil to reach

Courtesy of Stokes Seed Co.

Castor oil beans are excellent annual plants for hiding eyesores

the permanent water level.

When you look at an evergreen, it is hard to realize that evaporation goes on through the needles of the trees all the time. By "all the time", we mean all seasons of the year,

Alyssum makes a fine edging for the foundation bed

Courtesy of A. B. Morse Co.

Photo by Malak, Ottawa—Courtesy of the Dutch Bulb Growers

Dwarf evergreens can be planted in some of the larger pockets of the rock garden for much needed winter color

Spring, Summer, Autumn and Winter. Naturally, the evaporation is much more rapid in July and early August. What happens is this — the roots take the moisture from the surrounding soil and move it up through the trunk and branches to the needles. If there is no moisture in the soil, the needles will dry out, turn brown and fall off. This is usually the end of the tree, and no effort on your part at that time will revive it.

It is during the first two years, and particularly the first one that evergreens need watering the most. It seems likely, however, that under the adverse growing conditions which exist in the average subdivision today, evergreens need watering for their entire life.

The thing to keep in mind is that the roots must be kept moist, but not constantly wet. You use the same practise for watering evergreens as for the lawn and the rest of the garden. Frequent light sprinklings every day are useless and can actually harm the evergreens. It is better to water once a week and let the moisture really soak into the ground. For evergreens it is best to remove the nozzle of the hose and allow a small stream of water to soak into the soil around each tree until the soil will not absorb any more water. This usually takes at least two or three hours.

Another good way is to use one of the plastic or canvas soakers which are set out on the ground surrounding the evergreens and which gradually releases water at a rate

Courtesy of The Ontario Agricultural College, Guelph, Ont.

Evergreens can help to beautify a cemetery

watering, just because the lawns do not need it. On the other hand, it is accepted fact that the last watering you give the day before freeze-up time can be the most important of the whole year. Unless the rainfall in October and November is frequent and heavy, keep on soaking your evergreens every week until the ground is frozen solidly.

Feeding Evergreens—Like other plant life, evergreens, to be their best must be fed at regular intervals. Feeding will enhance the appearance of the trees and bushes, make them more vigorous and the needles will stay green. Evergreens are apt to be taken too much for granted and so are often neglected when it comes to feeding, thus many unwittingly are doomed to poor health and perhaps extinction.

Regular feeding is a must for any evergreen

Courtesy of Erindale Nurseries, Erindale, Ont.

the soil can absorb without any run-off.

In areas where there are water restrictions, and this happens only too frequently nowadays with the huge industrial demands for water, there is a gadget on the market which automatically will turn on the water late in the evening and shut it off at any given time during the night.

Having your evergreens go into the Winter with the roots dry can be just as harmful as lack of water during a hot July drought. Evaporation goes on continually through the needles of evergreens as we mentioned earlier. Even on a zero day the needles are still giving off moisture. This moisture was taken up from the soil by the roots and passed into the air through the needles.

Once October arrives, the tendency is to put away the hose and not do any more

Courtesy of A. B. Morse Co.

A foundation planting should consist of a balanced mixture of evergreens, shrubs and flowers

Established evergreens require feeding in April and again in either July or August.

Use one half pound of complete plant food or fertilizer per foot of height of the tree. The best way to apply the fertilizer to the smaller evergreens is to dig a shallow trench around the outer spread of the branches. Sprinkle in the fertilizer at the one-half pound per foot rate and cover with soil. The rain, or the next time you water, will carry the fertilizer down to the roots.

It is possible to improve older evergreens by feeding. The best way to give them plant food is to use the same method as you would for feeding a shade tree. Just beyond the outer spread of the branches dig a series of holes, at least 18 inches deep, and about two inches in diameter. You can make the

holes with an ordinary crowbar or an earth auger. There are several earth augers on the market which will do a good job, and if you have trees, it is advisable to buy one

There is only room for 5 or 6 evergreens in front of the average sized house.

Courtesy of The Ontario Horticultural Assoc.

Courtesy of The Ontario Horticultural Assoc.

Here's what happens when an evergreen is planted too close to a set of steps

as part of your regular garden tool equipment. They are simple to use and the cost will be small compared to the returns your trees will make in the way of greater beauty of color and form, as well as increased growth and vigor.

There are two ways of doing the actual feeding. One is to fill the holes with a mixture consisting of half complete fertilizer and half dry soil or sand. The other method is to use one of the new "stick form" complete fertilizers. All you need do is make the holes as above and insert the sticks.

There may be other reasons for the lack of health of your evergreens. The abundant use of fertilizer certainly will not solve all evergreen troubles. For instance, it will not be able to counteract the bad effects of the lack of watering, a poor planting location, or too much shade.

For fertilizer, many people advocate the

use of bone meal. In fact, they swear by it. You must remember that bone meal, which is high in phosphorous, is very slow-acting and will remain in the soil a long time before the evergreens receive any benefit from it. In any case, it is only one part of the three plant food elements the various shrubs, trees and evergreens need for top-notch growth. They also need nitrogen and potash to help them do their best. This is why a complete fertilizer containing all three plant food elements is always a much better bet for the home gardener.

Winter Protection

Many persons do not realize that evergreens in the garden need to have some winter protection. This is particularly true for those newly planted. You may argue evergreens in the woods do not receive any winter protection. While it is true they do not receive any man-made shields from the onslaughts of the cold wintry winds, they do get generally adequate protection from nature.

Our needle-bearing evergreens such as the Mugho pine, cedar, juniper, and yew which make up the bulk of our foundation and garden plantings will certainly need some form of protection.

Winter damage to evergreens can happen in two ways. First of all, the weight of snow on the branches after a storm can break many of them unless the snow is shaken from the evergreens right after the snowfall.

Choose low-growing evergreens for planting beneath windows.

Courtesy of A. B. Morse Co.

Courtesy of The Ontario Horticultural Assoc.

**Make a tour of the garden after every snow storm and shake the branches
to dislodge the snow**

Ice storms in February or March can be particularly damaging, not only because the weight of the ice breaks down the branches, but if it turns sunny immediately after the storm the ice will act as a magnifying glass causing severe burning and browning of the evergreen needles. Pyramidal cedars in the foundation planting and shrub borders, and cedar hedges are often seriously affected this way.

It is unfortunate that evergreens do not recover from damage in the same manner as do shrubs. If a forsythia is broken, new growth starts from the old wood behind the break and soon covers any damage. Evergreens, on the other hand, rarely put out young growth from the old wood and if they do, it usually takes a long time.

Members of the yew family are able to start new wood, but even with them it takes

two or three years to cover up the original break. With evergreens, all new growth is produced from the tips of the shoots, or from buds on the side shoots of the previous year's growth. If a branch is broken leaving a bare stub, it will always remain that way and become hidden only after a period of time by young growth produced by surrounding branches.

This is also a good reason to be careful with the pruners. Mistakes in pruning evergreens will be there to haunt you for years to come.

It is a good plan after every snow storm to make a methodical tour of the garden, shaking the branches to dislodge the snow. This should be done the next morning after a snow storm or within 24 hours at the latest. Otherwise, the snow will be frozen fairly solidly and will be practically im-

Mistakes in pruning can haunt you for years to come

Be sure and use a sharp knife or pruners for any trimming

Blue spruces are one of the best evergreens if planted in the right location

Courtesy of The Ontario Horticultural Assoc.

Courtesy of Province of Quebec—Dept. of Travel

Evergreens in the woods are protected against the hot summer sun by a thick natural mulch

possible to dislodge from the branches.

The best way of protecting evergreens is to erect a burlap screen on the south and west sides of the trees especially in the case of new plantings. We do this to cut down the damaging action of the winter winds and sun. Be sure to put the burlap screens in place before the ground freezes solid, or they will not be firm enough to withstand the wind for several months. An excellent method for doing this is to erect a frame of stout stakes driven firmly into the soil and then fix the burlap securely to the stakes. This is certainly preferable to wrapping the plants individually, although there may be isolated cases when the latter method would be necessary.

Avoid being too eager to remove the winter protection in the early Spring, even though the weather appears bright and the screens seem unsightly. There is more damage done to evergreens during the late Winter and early Spring by the sun and wind than during the really cold months of January and February.

Winter Mulching—In the colder parts of North America once the ground has frozen solidly, it is advisable to place a thick mulch of hay, straw, well-rotted barn-yard manure, discarded mushroom manure or peat moss around each evergreen. Make this mulch 8 to 10 inches deep and have it extend at least two or three feet beyond the outer spread of the branches. The lighter materials such as hay, straw or peat moss will have to be weighted with a thin covering of earth, light pieces of lumber or tree branches to prevent the mulch from blowing away.

Such a mulch should be placed around Fall planted evergreens in all but the warmest locations.

Why do we apply such a mulch? It prevents the soil from thawing and freezing during alternate cold and warm spells.

Since the ground stays frozen hard, the wind will not be able to sway the trees back and forth and loosen the soil around the roots. During Winter, air pockets form which dry out the roots and kill the evergreens.

Most Evergreen Trees Drop Needles in the Fall—Fall is the time of year when most evergreens carry out "operation

A winter mulch prevents the soil from thawing and freezing during alternate cold and warm spells

Courtesy of The Canadian National Railways

needle drop". Pines and spruces drop one year's growth of needles in the early Fall. In Scotch pines, the 3-year old needles turn yellowish and then fall off. The red pine usually drops its 4-year old needles, while white pine normally keeps only 1 or 2 year's growth of needles.

The needles which are lost are those nearest the center of the tree. The younger, green needles are at the ends of the branches.

While this shedding operation is in progress, the trees often appear to be dead or dying. However, as soon as a hard wind or heavy rain occurs, the old needles are knocked to the ground and the tree again appears normal.

Unusual Summer seasons of drought or heavy rains may upset this natural process and cause more than the normal number of needles to drop. In these cases, if the tree keeps the current year's needles in a green healthy condition the tree will continue to grow next year.

Cones and Seeds of Evergreens— Out in King's County, California, not too many miles from Fresno is the Sequoia National Forest. As might be expected, here grow the giant Sequoias which we previously have mentioned were in full growth when Moses walked the earth, and which remain healthy to this day.

Visitors to this forest expect the cones

Most evergreens drop their needles in the fall

Courtesy of The Canadian National Railways

Courtesy of New Brunswick Dept. of Travel

The cones of evergreens also come in a variety of colors

produced by the Sequoia to be in direct proportion to their tremendous size. They often pick up large pine cones measuring as much as 20 inches in length and 3 to 4 inches in diameter thinking they grow on a Sequoia tree. This is a mistake because it acutally comes from the sugar pine. The Sequoia or redwood produces small cones, usually no more than 3 inches long and $1\frac{1}{2}$ inches in diameter.

So you see, the size of the cone does not bear any relation whatsoever to the size of the tree. Cones vary in size from the tiny ones of the larch, which are about $\frac{1}{2}$ inch in length, to the 20 inch ones of the sugar pine.

We have previously mentioned in this book that evergreens come in many colors

other than the traditional green. Their cones also vary in color, usually depending on the different stages of growth. They can be blue, green, violet, brown, gold or even bright yellow.

Junipers do not produce cones, but seeds in the form of berries. These berries are round and sometimes have a white, blue or even pinkish tint, and are about the size of a garden pea. On the other hand, the members of the yew family develop red berries, each of which contains a seed. In the odd case, the berries can be yellow instead of red in color.

Some cones are extremely long lasting and have been known to remain on the trees for as long as six or seven years. Others fall off after one or two years at the most. There are cones which have been designed by nature to seemingly explode, and thus scatter their seeds over a wide area. Other types are so tightly closed that they will preserve their seeds through a forest fire.

Courtesy of A. B. Morse Co.

The Yew or Taxus family is the finest evergreen for foundation planting purposes

MOST POPULAR EVERGREENS

THE YEW (Taxus)

The yew family is without a doubt the finest evergreen for foundation planting purposes and does the best of any evergreen in shady conditions.

The various members of the yew family are no recent find or introduction in evergreens for we have been growing them in our gardens in many parts of the world for hundreds of years.

The Romans had a particular liking for the yews and freely planted them in their gardens. It was they who gave the family its botanical name of "Taxus".

However, the Romans were not the only ones to admire and grow this outstanding family of evergreens, for in Japan gardeners have been using them to create beauty around temples and homes for centuries.

The famed English longbow was made

When half the hole has been filled in with soil and firmed, fill it up with water and let it drain completely away before adding the rest of the soil

Courtesy of A. B. Morse Co.

Members of the yew family can be pruned in much the same way as a privet hedge

Courtesy of Kelly Bros., Dansville, N.Y.

Upright Japanese Yew

from yew trees and was the mainstay of English armies before the invention of gun-powder and firearms. A journey around older gardens will reveal many figures carved in growing yews hundreds of years ago that are still alive and healthy to this day.

Recommended Varieties:

Japanese Yew (Upright, Taxus Cuspidata) (8 to 10 feet)—We can thank the Japanese for the development of one of the best of the ornamental evergreens. In 1861 the Japanese yew was first introduced to North America from Japan.

Like the other members of the yew family, the upright Japanese variety will survive and even grow reasonably well in

Members of the yew family grow quite well in the smoky and dusty city conditions

Courtesy of A. B. Morse Co.

the smoky and dusty conditions found in our larger cities. It has a beautiful pyramidal form with deep green foliage and makes an ideal evergreen for softening the corner of a house. The dense foliage has a remarkable ability to withstand heavy pruning and close shearing. The Upright Japanese yew is in a class by itself for foundation plantings, clipped specimen evergreens and hedges.

Japanese Yew (Spreading, Taxus Cuspidata) (3 to 4 feet) — This is the spreading form of the Japanese yew which usually grows more wider than its height. It branches out from the bottom with several stems which develop into a bush form. It produces rich, dark green foliage with

Courtesy of Kelly Bros., Dansville, N.Y.

Spreading Japanese Yew

numerous crimson red berries appearing in the Fall. The spreading Japanese yew trims very easily and forms a dense very desir-

The spreading Japanese yew makes a fine hedge

Courtesy of A. B. Morse Co.

Courtesy of A. B. Morse Co.

Hick's yew is the best all-purpose evergreen for the home garden

Hick's Yew

The growth is upright, with a rich, dark glossy green foliage which is resistant to extreme heat and cold. It will grow either in sun or shade and makes an ideal evergreen for the north side of the house or other similar locations. It can be allowed to grow in its natural columnar way or trimmed into almost any shape. Hick's yew is by far the darkest green of any evergreen available. It is also the hardiest and the easiest to transplant of any of the yew family. It will grow 6 to 8 feet in height at maturity, but if trimmed regularly can be kept to any height over three feet. There seems to be little doubt that this variety will make the best possible evergreen hedge. Its numerous branches ascend almost vertically, although there is an excellent main stem.

An excellent contrast can be achieved

able and attractive evergreen for planting under windows, and at the base of taller growing trees such as the pyramidal cedar. This evergreen flourishes in sunny and northern exposures.

Yew Hick's Pyramidal (Taxus Hicksi) (6 to 8 feet) — One of the first evergreens to choose when landscaping your garden should be Hick's yew. It is probably the best all-purpose evergreen that can be grown.

The growth of Hick's yew is upright

A dwarf Japanese yew is the hardiest and the dwarfest

by planting a golden spreading juniper side by side with a Hick's yew. The former is very similar in habit of growth and appearance to the popular Pfitzer's juniper except for its bright golden needles.

Dwarf Japanese Yew (Taxus Cuspidata Nana) (3 to 4 feet) — Here is the hardiest and the smallest of all the yews which has a remarkable ability to withstand both shade and a dusty smoky atmosphere. A little judicious pruning from time to time will keep it small enough so that it becomes an ideal evergreen for planting in large pockets in the rock garden or in foundation plantings and other areas where a dwarf tree is desirable.

Brown's Yew (Taxus Browni) (3 to 4 feet) — Brown's yew is a semi-upright vase-shaped evergreen with waxy green foliage. It is more compact, slower growing and requires less pruning than the Japanese yew. It is easily trimmed and makes a most attractive evergreen for planting almost anywhere in the garden, particularly in foundation plantings.

JUNIPER (Juniperus)

This family contains the largest group of hardy evergreens able to be grown in the garden. Not only will they thrive where

Brown's yew requires very little pruning

Courtesy of Sheridan Nurseries, Islington, Ont.

Courtesy of Sheridan Nurseries, Islington, Ont.

Do not remove the burlap sacking before planting

the climate is cold, but will grow equally well in the warmer parts of North America.

Home gardeners everywhere favor junipers in the garden because they come in practically all the evergreen shapes, from bushy spreading plants to the tall thin columnar types.

Junipers like a location where they will get lots of sunshine and where the soil is not too heavy. Heavier clay soils can be prepared for planting this class of evergreens by digging in quantities of humus. All the junipers can be kept relatively small if need be, because they are easily pruned.

SPREADING JUNIPERS
Recommended Varieties:

Spreading Juniper (Juniperus Pfitzeriana) (4 to 5 feet spread) — There is

Courtesy of Kelly Bros., Dansville, N.Y.

Pfitzer's juniper

is unlike most other members of the juniper family because it will stand considerable shade, although it does its best in full sunshine. It is an excellent variety for planting underneath windows, as an accent plant at the base of tall growing trees and makes a most attractive entrance planting.

Blue Pfitzer Juniper (Juniperus Pfitzeriana Glauca) (4 to 5 feet spread) — This blue beauty is of great value in the garden. It resembles the popular green Pfitzer juniper mentioned above in every way except that it grows more compactly and the foliage is a delightful steel blue all year round. You will certainly admire the dense feathery foliage and the beautiful effect it creates in the Wintertime when

no doubt that the green Pfitzer's juniper is the most popular and widely planted of all the spreading evergreens. Healthy and vigorous dark green foliage is produced on a compact spreading plant. This evergreen

The golden tipped Pfitzer's juniper makes a wonderful contrast

Courtesy of A. B. Morse Co.

Courtesy of Sheridan Nurseries, Islington, Ont.

Golden tipped Pfitzer's juniper has a 4 to 5 foot spread

there is practically no other color in the foundation planting or the rest of the garden.

Golden Tipped Pfitzer's Juniper (Juniperus Pfitzeriana Aurea) (4 to 5 feet spread) — This is a delightful novelty

Junipers form the largest group of evergreens for the home garden

Courtesy of Patmore Nurseries, Brandon, Manitoba

worthy of a place in any garden. Each year the new growth has brilliant yellow tips framing the dark green foliage. It makes a wonderful color contrast if planted between blue or green colored evergreens. There is no need to worry about its hardiness.

Old Gold Pfitzer Juniper (Juniperus Pfitzeriana Old Gold) (2 to 3 feet spread) — Is a slow growing more compact form of the Golden Pfitzer whose gold tipped branches keep their color all Winter long. It would be hard to find a more useful and more attractive low-growing evergreen. There is no better evergreen for planting in the larger pockets of the rock garden where it will bring much needed Winter color.

Andorra Juniper (Juniperus Horizontalis Plumosa) (2 to 3 feet spread)—Still more Winter color is provided by the low-growing Andorra juniper. The foliage is a bluish green color in the Summer, turning to a most charming purplish green in the Winter. It grows only six to eight inches high and spreads out very quickly. This is the ideal evergreen for covering banks which are too steep to permit mowing of grass. Also it is an attractive evergreen

Old Gold Pfitzer's Juniper is a more compact form of the Golden Tipped

Courtesy of McConnell Nurseries, Port Burwell, Ont.

Courtesy of Sheridan Nurseries, Islington, Ont.

Pfitzer's juniper has a 4 to 5 foot spread

for the rock garden, foundation planting or for planting in clumps along the front of the mixed border where it will provide color in the Wintertime, at a time when none other is available.

Savin Juniper (Juniperus Savina) (3 to 4 feet spread) — This evergreen is very popular because of the low spreading form of its ascending branches and its consistently dark green needles which really stand out in the garden. It is a very compact evergreen requiring little trimming, and is hardy enough to stand the coldest Winters.

Blue Danube Juniper (Juniperus Blue Danube) (3 to 4 feet spread) — Here is a

fairly new evergreen which resembles the Savin juniper mentioned above, but having a more horizontal or flat habit of growth. The lovely and striking blue foliage combines well with other evergreens. It is especially fine when planted alongside a Golden Pfitzer juniper.

Blue Hetz Juniper (Juniperus Glauca Hetzi) (4 to 6 feet spread) — The Blue Hetz juniper is recognized as being the fastest growing of all the junipers. It closely resembles the green Pfitzer juniper except that the extra fine foliage is silvery blue in color and it is a much faster grower. This variety makes an excellent evergreen for the foundation planting if given an occasional pruning to keep it within bounds.

Tamarix Juniper (Juniperus Sabina Tamariscifolia) (3 to 4 feet spread) — The Tamarix juniper is a smaller form of the Savin juniper mentioned before, growing 8 to 12 inches in height. It features beautiful bright green foliage. It is an ideal evergreen for the front of the foundation planting and there need be little or no worry about its hardiness.

Hick's Savin Juniper (Juniperus Sabina Hicksi) (3 to 4 feet spread)—This

Try planting the Gold Tipped next to the Blue Danube juniper

Courtesy of Sheridan Nurseries, Islington, Ont.

The Blue Hetz variety is the fastest growing of all the Junipers

Courtesy of Sheridan Nurseries, Islington, Ont.

Juniper and Juniper berries

The Tamarix juniper is a smaller form of the Savin juniper

is a fairly new Juniper that has the same growing habit as the Savin juniper and is just as hardy. However, the foliage is a silvery blue-green, more lacy and finer than the ordinary Savin. The upright feathery branches are particularly eye-catching.

UPRIGHT JUNIPERS
Recommended Varieties:

Mountbatten Blue Juniper (Juniperus Mountbatten) (6 to 10 feet)—The Mountbatten juniper is a comparatively recent variety with a most delightful steel blue foliage. Its habit of growth is compact and pyramidal and does not require trimming. The beginner to gardening will value it because of its hardiness and rapid growth.

Red Cedar or Blue Virginian Juniper (Juniperus Virginiana Glauca) (6 to 12 feet) — This evergreen is a source of bewilderment to most people for despite its misleading name the red cedar is actually a juniper. It is one of our native evergreens and nature scattered it all over the North American continent from Canada to the Gulf of Mexico. It was one of the first evergreens to be grown in gardens on this continent. Those we buy from the nursery have an upright growth habit which is both

compact and pyramidal. The foliage is a rich silvery blue in the Summer but as Winter approaches the tips of the new foliage becomes a pinkish red in color. The red cedar requires some trimming, especially when small, to enable it to develop an attractive and compact habit of growth. It is an easily trimmed variety which combines well with other evergreens. Full sunshine and plenty of air circulation are its most important requirements. This is one of the few plants able to flourish in poor sandy or gravelly soil.

Myer's Juniper (Juniperus Squamata Meyeri) (4 to 5 feet)—Here we have an evergreen which is entirely different in habit, color and form. This beautiful vase-shaped juniper has an unusual foliage which is much admired. Its color is a

The Mountbatten juniper has delightful steel blue foliage

**The Mountbatten blue juniper grows
6 to 10 feet high**

**The color of Meyers juniper is a striking
blend of green, white and pinkish-red**

striking blend of green, white and pinkish
red. Because of its shape, color and extreme
hardiness, it has many valuable uses in the
garden.

Myer's Juniper Wilsoni (Juniperus
Squamata Wilsoni) (4 to 5 feet)—This
variety has the same upright bushy form
and other characteristics of the Myer
juniper mentioned above, but the foliage is
a fine bluish green in color.

Spiny Greek Juniper (Juniperus
Excelsa Stricta) (4 to 5 feet)—The Spiny
Greek juniper is a superb quick growing
beauty which rapidly attains a height of
3½ feet before slowing to mature. It has a
most delightful dense columnar form with
steel blue foliage all year round. This is
another evergreen which does not require

**Myers juniper is entirely different in habit,
color and form**

Courtesy of Sheridan Nurseries, Islington, Ont.

Spiny Greek juniper is a quick-growing beauty

Courtesy of Sheridan Nurseries, Islington, Ont.

Hills Dundee juniper is a very rapid grower and requires very little pruning

trimming. It can be planted in almost any part of the garden to provide stately beauty every month of the year.

Hill's Dundee Juniper (Juniperus Virginia Hilli) (6 to 10 feet) — Hill's Dundee juniper is a most attractive blue-green color in the Summer, turning to a lovely purplish-green in the Winter. It is a good evergreen to plant for immediate effect because it is a very rapid grower and requires little trimming. This makes it a favorite among beginners and for new gardens. Left to its own devices it usually throws a number of stems from the ground forming an erect bush. However, by limiting the growth to one stem, a fine upright form can easily be produced.

Blaauws Blue Vase Juniper (Juni-

peruss Blaauws variety) (4 to 5 feet)—This is one of the newest varieties and is an excellent dwarf vase-shaped evergreen. The most delightful blue foliage and vase form will soon win many friends. This is not an evergreen to plant in the shade because it needs a sunny location in which to grow its best. Hardiness is no problem and wherever it is planted in the garden it will bring extra color and delight.

CEDARS OR ARBORVITAES

The arborvitaes are an extremely hardy group of evergreens and are used in gardens everywhere. One group or species of this evergreen is native to North America while others are found in Asian countries, notably China, Japan and Korea. Both the American and the Asian kinds have numerous members to their respective

Courtesy of Sheridan Nurseries, Islington, Ont.

Blaauws juniper is an excellent dwarf vased-shaped evergreen

families.

Recommended Varieties:

Pyramidal Cedar (Thuja Occidentalis Pyramidalis) (8 to 10 feet) — This pyramidal evergreen is one of the most popular, and is the type most often used in gardens. It is a beautiful dense growing tree which grows in an erect columnar way. Its height at maturity is an advantage as it enables the tree to be used equally well in foundation, porch and bed plantings. It is very narrow and erect with a fine compact habit. Color is a lush, lovely dark green. To get best results, make sure that you plant it where it will get lots of sunshine.

American Cedar or Arborvitae (Thuja Occidentalis) (20 to 25 feet) —

The pyramidal cedar is one of the most popular evergreens in the home garden

Courtesy of Sheridan Nurseries, Islington, Ont.

Courtesy of Kelly Bros., Dansville, N.Y.

Pyramidal Arbor-Vitae

The False Cypress and Cypress cone

Courtesy of A. B. Morse Co.

Pyramidal cedars are fine for planting on each side of the entrance-way

**Little Champion is a fast growing
globe-shaped cedar**

This is the native cedar which grows in
many parts of North America. Most of the
evergreen hedges which have been planted
in Eastern gardens during the last half
century have been composed of this hardy
native cedar. It is a very versatile evergreen which can be trained either as a
low hedge from 3 to 4 feet in height, or
one as high as 10 to 12 feet. This type
of hedge is very susceptible to damage from
ice storms. As mentioned earlier in the
book a storm in late February or early
March will coat the needles with ice and
when the sun comes out will act as a
magnifying glass and seriously brown the
leaves.

Cedars are found growing naturally in
moist, often swampy ground, and so should
not be planted in very dry soils. It is a
good plan to lay one of the canvas or plastic

**Little Gem, also known as Little Champ, is
fine for the larger pockets of the
rock garden**

soakers along the bottom of the hedge and
let the water gradually soak into the
ground for several hours. In periods when
there is little or no rainfall, it is good
practise to do this once a week to create
the moist conditions in which the tree grows
naturally. Moisture also helps to maintain
the bright grassy green color of the foliage.

Wares Siberian Arborvitae (Thuja
Wareana) (6 to 10 feet) — Here we have
an extremely hardy evergreen which will
stand the coldest climates, but requires a
sunny location for best growth. It is
a strong compact grower of graceful
pyramidal form. When making your landscaping plans, this evergreen should be

Globe Arbor-Vitae

Thuja Orientalis, a compact pyramidal cedar whose finely cut foliage is a bright golden color

considered for the corner of the medium sized or large house. Color is a lovely grass green.

Little Champion Arborvitae (Thuja Occidentalis Little Champion) (2½ to 3 feet) — Little Champion is a superb hardy globe cedar first introduced in 1957. It is a fast growing, very hardy, globe shaped variety with a most pleasing green color. It requires no trimming and retains its rich naturally thick globe shape without shearing.

SPRUCE (Picea)

Spruces are one of the most important evergreens in Canada and the northern part of the United States. The family embraces a large number of forms. Many of these trees are grown as magnificent lawn or park specimens while others are most suitable for hedges, windbreaks and general mass planting. There are also dwarf forms suitable for rock gardens and small borders which will maintain a dwarf, dense compact shape indefinitely.

They like the cold weather, so much so that some types are found growing inside the Arctic Circle. Pines will thrive in the warmer climates, but the spruces are not very much at home in the heat. They usually fail to grow well south of Oklahoma. While most varieties of spruces are native to the United States and Canada, there are some excellent types which have been imported to our gardens from Japan, Korea and other

Evergreens make wonderful windbreaks

Courtesy of Canadian Government Travel Bureau, Ottawa, Canada

Spruce and Spruce cone

Courtesy of Nova Scotia Travel Bureau

Pines will thrive in warm climates, but spruces are not at home in the heat

Courtesy of Patmore Nurseries, Brandon, Manitoba

It is a mistake to plant blue spruce in the middle of the lawn

The Koster blue spruce is the most beautiful of all evergreens

Courtesy of Sheridan Nurseries, Islington, Ont.

Asiatic countries.

We have been growing spruces for hundreds of years, so it is no wonder there is a wide variety from which to choose. They vary in size from dwarf kinds growing little more than 2 feet high, to veritable giants which eventually reach 120 or more feet in height. This is why it is necessary before making a purchase at the nursery or garden center to be sure to find out how high any of the spruces or other evergreens will be at maturity. It is only then you can make the correct decision as to a suitable location.

Recommended Varieties:

Koster Blue Spruce (Picea Pungence Kosteriana) (30 to 40 feet)—This is one of the most spectacular, finest and valuable of

The Colorado spruce is a popular evergreen for lawn specimen planting

Courtesy of Horticultural Experiment Station, Vineland, Ont.

The Koster blue and other spruces cannot be repressively pruned

bed with a large number of golden yellow trumpet daffodils. The next Spring you will have color beyond your wildest dreams with the brilliant blue color of the needles contrasting sharply from the golden yellow of the daffodils. Once the daffodils have finished flowering, they can be replaced by any of the tall growing, large flowered, yellow colored marigolds. The best strains for this purpose would be Yellow Climax or Golden Climax.

When the middle of September arrives, the marigolds will no doubt be fading away, and can be replaced by some of the yellow-flowered hardy chrysanthemums, which can be moved from the nursery or another part of the garden in bud or in full flower without harm or set-back. The chrysanthemums could be grown in the vegetable or cutting garden and transferred to the bed surround-

The popularity of the Blue Spruce is due mainly to its graceful form and brilliant glistening color

Courtesy of McConnell Nurseries, Port Burwell, Ont.

all lawn specimen evergreens. Its popularity is due mainly to its graceful form and brilliant, glistening silvery blue color.

Unless you have a very large garden or a small estate, you will have to keep the Koster Blue spruce and any of the other blues to the side or back of the garden. One of the most common mistakes is to plant them on either side of the front sidewalk, about 15 feet from the house. Before long the trees will be 12 to 15 feet tall, and if left undisturbed will rapidly climb skyward. Such trees cannot be repressively pruned.

Those of you who have a Blue spruce already growing in your garden can create an eye-catching and tremendously colorful display by extending the bed surrounding the tree three or four feet beyond the outer spread of the branches. In the Fall fill the ing the Blue spruce about the middle of September. Some of the new giant-flowered Harvest mums would be ideal for this purpose.

For trees that have been in for 10 or more years and are 15 to 20 feet in height, a group of forsythia (golden bells) shrubs will also provide an exciting splash of late April and early May color.

You may ask about young trees that have just been planted. Naturally, the beds surrounding these would only extend about 2 feet beyond the outer spread of the branches, and the trumpet daffodils and other tall growing flowers would be out of proportion to the size of the Blue spruce. Here, you could plant golden yellow cro-

Courtesy of Sheridan Nurseries, Islington, Ont.

The Nest spruce forms a low dense shrub resembling a pin cushion

cuses and have the same striking color effect. These could be followed by the extremely dwarf growing Petite Gold or

Leave enough room in the foundation planting for annuals, chrysanthemums and other flowers

Courtesy of Bristol Nurseries Inc., Bristol, Conn.

Courtesy of The Geo. J. Ball Inc., West Chicago, Ill.

Giant Harvest Mums can be moved to the foundation bed when in full bloom

**Dwarf marigold Spun Gold, Red Satin, Maytime, Glitters and Paleface petunias
combine with evergreens for a fine show**

**Norway spruce makes a fine ornamental
tree or windbreak**

Petite Yellow marigolds which won a recent
All-America Award. You could also use
Spun Gold, the 1960 All-America winner in
the marigolds which produces big flowers
on short stalky plants. Around the middle
of September these could also be replaced
with some of the low-growing yellow cushion chrysanthemums.

Blue Colorado Spruce (Picea Pungence Glauca) (30 to 40 feet)—Here is an
especially fine evergreen which will add
beauty and value to your property. While
their foliage is extra fine silvery blue, it
must be admitted it is not quite as intense a
blue as the Koster. On the other hand, the
Colorado Blue spruce usually makes a
slightly better shaped tree. It is very ele-

Courtesy of Patmore Nurseries, Brandon, Manitoba

Shearing takes away the natural beauty from a Koster blue spruce

Courtesy of Ontario Horticultural Assoc.

Evergreens have many uses in the rock garden

Courtesy of Nova Scotia Travel Bureau

Evergreens can be enjoyed in nature and in the garden

gant when planted as a lawn specimen tree in groups of two or three, or as a tall windbreak.

DWARF VARIETIES

One of the difficulties in planting most evergreens in the larger pockets in the rock garden is to keep them confined to the pocket. They also tend to over-run the foundation planting surrounding smaller homes. A check through your nursery catalog will show that there are several kinds of dwarf spruces which will not only stay permanently dwarf, but at the same time will maintain a dense compact shape without clipping.

Hedgehog Spruce (Abies Gregoriana Veitchi) (2 to 3 feet) — You will admire the dwarf mound-like form and compactness of this evergreen. Color is an attractive green.

Courtesy of The Ontario Agricultural College, Guelph, Ont.

The Norway spruce is a magnificent park specimen tree

Nest Spruce (Abies Nidiformis) (2 to 3 feet) — An extremely low-growing and worthwhile variety which forms a low, dense shrub resembling a nest or pincushion. The branches grow close together in tight layers and form an almost impenetrable head. There is hardly any evergreen which grows slower than the Nest spruce. It averages about 1 inch of growth a year.

Dwarf White Spruce (Glauca Conica) (3 feet)—Is another extremely slow growing compact evergreen of the pyramidal type. Foliage is an attractive grass green.

Norway Spruce (Picea Excelsa) (80 feet) — This familiar evergreen is widely planted not only in Europe, but in Canada and the United States. Many fine varieties have been developed for ornamental uses and it is excellent as a specimen tree for larger gardens, for windbreaks or park planting. The branches are quite stiff when

Courtesy of Canadian Government Travel Bureau, Ottawa, Canada

Typical farm land in Cape Breton

By Armstrong Roberts

The lawn, trees and foundation planting help to give the house a look of permanence

young, but becoming pendulous and droopy as the tree matures. The Norway spruce is extremely tolerant of soil conditions, and

will grow in both damp and dry locations. However, the soil must be well-drained. It is also quite tolerant of a sunny or shady

A bird bath helps to attract the birds to the garden

Courtesy of The Ontario Agricultural College, Guelph, Ont.

Tall growing evergreens like the spruces should be kept to the sides and back of the garden

Courtesy of The Ontario Agricultural College, Guelph, Ont.

location. The best use for this evergreen is as a windbreak.

White Spruce (Picea Abies Glauca) (60 to 70 feet) — The White spruce is a very handsome specimen tree becoming spire-like with age. Foliage is a most attractive blue-green in color. This evergreen is not too particular about whether it is planted in heavy or light, damp or dry soils.

It must have a location in full sun, and there it will withstand plenty of heat and dry weather.

PINE (Pinus)

Mention of the word "pine", and the first thing to come to mind is evergreen. Many of the members of this group are suitable only for lumbering purposes, but fortunately for our gardens there are a number

Combination of needle and broad leaf evergreens shows off this English style home to perfection

Courtesy of G. Hamilton

Courtesy of A. B. Morse Co.

Many pines, like Pinus Strobus, make fine ornamental evergreens

Pine and Pine cone

White pines make an excellent windbreak

which have a definite place as ornamentals. Pines only thrive in plenty of light and sunshine, so if your garden is shady, this is not the place to plant any of the pines. They also prefer a light, sandy or gravelly soil in which to grow.

It won't be long before these evergreens will overrun the foundation bed

Lawns and foundation planting blend the house into the landscape

Courtesy of Sheridan Nurseries, Islington, Ont.

**The Mugho pine is extremely valuable for the front of the foundation bed,
or the larger pockets in the rock garden**

Mugho Pine or Candle Pine (Pinus mughus) (2 to 4 feet)—Here we have an extremely valuable evergreen for planting either in the foundation beds or in the larger pockets in the rock garden. It originally came to North America from the mountainous sections of northern Europe. This evergreen features a dense globe shape with foliage which is a rich, bright green. All that is needed to maintain this valuable evergreen in a dwarf, compact form is a little pruning every year. The new growth each season is a greyish white in color, and makes the Mugho pine look for all the world as if it were a birthday cake covered with candles and given a green icing. By late June, the new growth will have developed as much as it will in the one year, and at this time the shoots should be pinched back. The soft young shoots should be

Courtesy of The Ontario Agricultural College, Guelph, Ont.

Swiss Pine

Courtesy of Nova Scotia Travel Bureau

The man who enjoys evergreens while fishing can also enjoy them in his garden

Courtesy of The Ontario Agricultural College, Guelph, Ont.

The Scotch pine is widely used as a Christmas tree

reduced to half their length in the case of newly planted Mugho pines. This will mean that your evergreen will be a perfectly symmetrical ball of green foliage.

A tall Japanese yew with two Mugho pines at its base makes an ideal combination for use as a foundation planting.

Austrian Pine (Pinus Nigra) (30 to 60 feet)—There is no doubt that the Austrian pine is one of the most excellent and handsome evergreens for this part of the world. Its compact habit, bright green glossy foliage and rapid growth make it extremely popular as a lawn specimen tree, windbreaks, and a mass planting. It prefers a sunny location.

Courtesy of The Canadian National Railways

Jasper Park Lodge

Courtesy of Nova Scotia Travel Bureau

A pastoral scene in Nova Scotia

Courtesy of Stokes Seed Co.

Garden beauty is created by a combination of evergreens and annuals

Scotch Pine (Pinus Silvestrus) (30 to 60 feet) — This is the evergreen used so much during the past few years for Christmas trees. Young married couples who have just started to have a family and who have a fair size garden can have a lot of fun planting two or three Scotch pines as each child is born. Then by the time the children are six or seven years old, they will have their very own Christmas tree. In growing them as Christmas trees, they should be planted 3 x 3 feet apart. However, in order to have a well shaped symmetrical tree, some pruning will have to be done the second or third year after planting, and continued annually until the tree is cut.

Western Yellow Pine (Ponderosa) (70 to 100 feet in the east)—This evergreen is the one covering the rolling hills and mountainsides of the west.

This tall growing pine becomes very pic-

Courtesy of City of Winnipeg

Evergreen landscape

Courtesy of the Nova Scotia Travel Bureau

Pines in the evening

turesque with age and is exceptionally useful for windbreaks. It prefers a sunny open location and a deep well-drained soil.

White Pine (Pinus Strobus) (100 to 120 feet)—The white pine is the beautiful native pine of the Canadian woods and is a very handsome ornamental specimen tree. It also makes a very good windbreak. White pine likes sun, but dislikes the smoky and dusty atmosphere of large cities. It is tolerant of soil conditions, providing the earth has a good moisture holding capacity and yet is well-drained.

HEMLOCK (Tsuga)

The ornamental hemlocks we grow in our gardens are either the Canadian or the Caroline hemlock. These trees have a delightful grace and very drooping and flowing

Canadian hemlock always has soft textured foliage

Courtesy of A. B. Morse Co.

Hemlock branch and hemlock cone

branches. They have the ability to do well in the shade and they make an ideal evergreen hedge. Main thing to watch in choosing a location for hemlocks is protection from the late Winter sun. This becomes more and more of a problem the further south you go.

Courtesy of Kelly Bros., Dansville, N.Y.

Canadian hemlock makes a fine tall hedge for suburban and rural areas

Canadian Hemlock (Tsuga Canadensis) (70 to 100 feet) — The soft texture of the foliage of this native evergreen has always made it a favorite for ornamental planting. It is also very useful as a tall hedge in sheltered positions in suburban or rural areas. The best location for this graceful tree is in partial shade where the soil is not too dry. This is not an evergreen to plant in light sandy or gravelly soil.

Carolina Hemlock (Tsuga Caroliniana) (70 feet)—This evergreen has a very

handsome and graceful form and makes a very fine ornamental specimen tree. Unfortunately, it is not as hardy as it might be. For instance, it is hardy in New England, but not reliably so in Northern Illinois. It is advisable to check with your local nurseryman or garden club before you buy, or allow a landscape man to plant it for you. If your garden is quite shady, the Carolina hemlock can be the answer to your problem. It likes a rich, moist soil, so do not plant it in a light, sandy or gravelly one. Where it is hardy, it makes a very fine tall hedge.

Courtesy of Sheridan Nurseries, Islington, Ont.

Hemlocks will grow 70 ft. or more in height

JAPANESE DWARF EVERGREENS

Many persons find the Japanese art of dwarfing evergreens most fascinating when

Courtesy of the Nova Scotia Travel Bureau

Pines on the coast

seeing it displayed at flower shows and exhibitions and wonder if they could do it in their own homes. Japanese gardeners have been able to produce gnarled and twisted evergreens in pots which are truly remarkable. Some miniature trees are so perfect that except for their size they could not be distinguished from their life-sized relatives.

Space is extremely limited in Japan not only for gardening but for living and this has no doubt led their gardeners to grow these miniature evergreens. With the traditional Japanese love of beauty, they have produced trees which are a joy to see.

When first seeing these miniature trees they appear to be hundreds of years old. Some of them are, but the majority have been developed in a few seasons' growth.

The average home gardener armed with the necessary knowledge can also produce these charming miniature evergreens.

First of all you need to select the correct

Picea Ohlendorfi, an ideal dwarf spruce for the foundation and rock garden planting

Courtesy of Sheridan Nurseries, Islington, Ont.

Courtesy of G. Hamilton

Before you plant, find out how high and how broad an evergreen will be at maturity

evergreens for the job. Cypress, cedars and pines can all be successfully grown as dwarf trees.

In talks with various experts, they agree that the easiest way for the average home gardener to produce a dwarf tree is to prune the roots heavily. Naturally, you will have to leave enough roots so that the seedling will remain healthy.

Notice we said seedling. The evergreens used for this purpose would be small seed-lings 4 to 6 inches high, and not the regular large specimens bought for landscaping purposes. Any reliable nurseryman should be able to arrange a supply for you. These should be inexpensive and you will be able to experiment with a number of seedlings to find out just how much of the root system can be pruned away without hurting the evergreen too much. From then on, it is just a matter of pruning heavily every time you repot. Incidentally, it is possible to grow one of these unique trees in an ordinary bulb pan, or in one of the dishes used for a cactus garden. The Japanese often make tiny slits in the bark which allows the twisting of the stems into various shapes. Wire or twine is also used to hold a twisted branch in place until it grows that way permanently. In some cases, leaves and branches are removed. In others, the branches and trunks of the trees are bent to

create the illusion of great age.

It is also advisable to help the aging and dwarfing process along by very lightly pruning back the tips of the branches each time you repot.

BROAD LEAVED EVERGREENS

In many industrial cities and towns, it is often difficult to grow the needle-leaved

Typical example of blue spruce planted too close together

Courtesy of G. Hamilton

Courtesy of A. B. Morse Co.

In the warmer parts the Daphne will keep its evergreen foliage from year to year

evergreens, such as juniper, cedar and pine. This is where the broad leaved evergreens come into their own. Also, many of them will provide an effective winter color. Quite

a number of these trees that retain their leaves in the Winter are very useful low-growing plants suitable for covering slopes, too steep to use a lawn mower, for ground cover under trees and for foundation plantings around the modern ranch style homes with windows down to floor level.

The garland flower has bright pink, delightfully fragrant flowers

Courtesy of Sheridan Nurseries, Islington, Ont.

DAPHNE (cenorum) — garland flower (15 inches) — This is a real gem for the garden having evergreen foliage which persists from year to year, but is seldom grown by home gardeners. The common name of this delightful broad-leaved evergreen is the garland flower. It has a spreading habit, growing 10 to 15 inches tall, and spreading to about 18 inches to 2 feet wide. The daphne produces

Courtesy of A. B. Morse Co.

Purple leaf wintercreeper Euonymous Fortunei Colorata

Winterberry Euonymus Radicans Erecta produces red berries late in the season

Courtesy of Kelly Bros., Dansville, N.Y.

bright pink, deliciously fragrant flowers. It is in bloom very early in the Spring and again in the Fall. There is not too much worry about its hardiness, except in areas where sub-zero temperatures are a common Winter occurrence. It needs a sunny, well-drained location, although it will do reasonably well in partial shade. Makes an excellent flowering shrub for the front of the mixed border, foundation planting, or in the larger pockets of the rock garden. It is fine for mixing with the needle leaved evergreens.

EVERGREEN EUONYMUS Winter Creeper (1½ to 5 feet)—This is a lovely group of plants which keep their bright

Courtesy of Sheridan Nurseries, Islington, Ont.

The Euonymus Emerald Charm has an upright columnar form

Courtesy of Sheridan Nurseries, Islington, Ont.

Euonymus Vegetus is best used as an evergreen vine for a wall

compact and is wonderful for narrow places in foundation plantings, porch entrances, as a hedge plant or as a specimen in formal plantings.

Euonymus Emerald Cushion (1½ to 2 feet) — This is the baby of the Euonymus family. It is a very dwarf shrub with dense compact habit and always retains its low wide outline with no tendency whatsoever to trail or climb. Lush green foliage crowds the plants all year, even in the Winter. It is an ideal broad leaved evergreen for the front of the border, foundation planting or in the large pockets of the rock garden. The leaves are a lovely dark green in color and leathery in texture during the growing

Euonymus Vegetus makes a fine ground cover under trees

Courtesy of Sheridan Nurseries, Islington, Ont.

evergreen foliage all year round. They require little or no trimming and are worthy of a place in any garden.

Recommended Varieties:

Corliss Hybrids—These four varieties are disease resistant, compact and bushy in habit, requiring no staking and little pruning. They have been under tests since 1934 and have survived dry Summers and severe Winters, with temperatures down to 20° below zero. The variety Emerald Cushion is not quite as hardy as the others.

Euonymus Emerald Charm (4 to 5 feet)—This handsome rather new variety has a beautiful upright columnar form with ascending branches and dark green glossy leaves. Will grow up to 5 feet high with a spread of 1½ feet. Grows dense and very

Courtesy of Sheridan Nurseries, Islington, Ont.

**Euonymus Emerald Pride grows 4 ft. high
and has a spread of 3½ feet**

season, and turn a bronze green in the
Winter time.

Euonymus Emerald Leader (3 to 4 feet) — This is a very distinctive variety

with an erect and shapely habit of growth,
rather bushy and at maturity will grow
4 feet high with a spread of 2½ feet. Forms
a neatly rounded bush with thick glossy
leaves. You will like the way the orange
colored fruits are produced in clusters. It
is superb in the foundation planting where
it combines well with evergreens of all
types. This evergreen is sure to brighten up
any landscape planting.

Euonymus Emerald Pride (4 feet) —

Here we have a neat, dwarf, compact shrub
almost as broad as it is tall, with heavy
foliage reaching right to the ground. Under
good soil conditions will grow to a height
of 4 feet with a spread of 3½ feet. This is
an unusually sturdy variety which is un-

Euonymus Radicans has lovely dark green leaves and fine red berries

Courtesy of A. B. Morse Co.

Courtesy of Sheridan Nurseries, Islington, Ont.

Euonymus Carrierei is very resisitant to smoke and shade

excelled for foundation plantings, or the shrub border. It is extremely useful as a specimen shrub where dwarf or semi-dwarf evergreens are desired.

Euonymus Fortunei Carrierei (3 feet) — This evergreen shrub with its lustrous green leaves should be planted for Winter effect. It grows into a mound 3 feet high and is very resistant to smoke and shade, and so makes a very good broad

Courtesy of A. B. Morse Co.

Euonymus Sarcoxie makes a fine specimen shrub in the foundation bed and the border

Courtesy of Bristol Nurseries Inc., Bristol, Conn.

Evergreens and chrysanthemums create a fine display

leaved evergreen for city plantings.

Euonymus Sarcoxie (3 feet) — One of the best of the broad leaved evergreens, has an excellent habit of growth, is very hardy and has beautiful dark green leaves. This makes a fine specimen evergreen in the shrub border or foundation planting, or as a medium height hedge.

Euonymus Vegetus (Climbs to 20 feet)

— This is at its best as an evergreen vine for walls, as a ground cover under trees, and as a low mound in the front of the foundation planting or mixed border. The beautiful lustrous green foliage is maintained all Winter long. It prefers a northern or eastern exposure and will grow in a wide variety of soil conditions.

HOLLIES (Ilex) — The following varieties of holly are reasonably hardy

Oregon Grape Holly is much hardier than the true holly. Thrives in shade and very easy to grow

maintaining their green foliage throughout the Winter. They are a welcome addition to our very short list of hardy broad-leaved evergreens.

Japanese Holly (Ilex Crenata) (3 to 4 feet) — This is a small growing holly which will be 4 feet at maturity and 3 feet across. The leaves are glossy and grow so thick you cannot see the twigs. It is very hardy and will grow either in alkaline or acid soil, in full sun or shade. Berries are black and the leaves are dark green in color and stay on the bushes throughout the Winter. It blends well with needle leaved evergreens or relieves the bareness of other shrubs when they have no leaves

All American mums at the Longwood Gardens

Courtesy of A. B. Morse Co.

English holly

during the Winter time.

Box Leaf Japanese Holly (Ilex Convexa) (4 feet) — Here we have another excellent evergreen shrub with shiny dark green, boxwood like foliage. It is excellent for planting in the foundation bed or in the shrub border.

Long-Stalk Holly (Ilex Pedunculosa) — The long-stalk holly is one of the hardiest of the evergreen hollies. The female plant bears red berries on long stalks.

KOREAN BOXWOOD (Boxus Koreana) (20 inches) — The Korean box

Courtesy of Kelly Bros., Dansville, N.Y.

The Pachysandra Terminalis makes a good ground cover

Cameo is one of the newer and better varieties of chrysanthemums

Courtesy of Bristol Nurseries Inc., Bristol, Conn.

Courtesy of A. B. Morse Co.

Where they are hardy the hollies make a fine show whether in leaf or in berry

Courtesy A. B. Morse Co.

The English Boxwood is not reliably hardy when the temperature falls to zero in the winter

is one of our most valuable broad leaved evergreens. This new variety increases its popularity every year because of its hardiness. If planted in good soil conditions, it will grow 20 inches high, but can be kept to almost any level by pruning. It makes a beautiful dwarf hedge, or is very useful as an edging evergreen. This is the plant to use in city areas because it easily withstands smoke, shade and insect pests. It can be trimmed to almost any shape. The Korean box also makes an excellent specimen plant in foundation beds or borders.

MOUNTAIN LAUREL (Kalmia Latifolia) (6 to 8 feet) — The Mountain

The Dawn Redwood is a most unusual tree recently re-introduced to North America from Central China

Courtesy of Kelly Bros., Dansville, N.Y.

Courtesy of A. B. Morse Co.

Big clusters of flowers cover the Mountain Laurel bushes

problem with this plant is its need for acid soil. Make the soil in which it is planted half peat moss and your plant should flourish.

YUCCA (Candle of our Lord or Adam's Needle) — Here we have a picturesque truly beautiful little grown perennial that keeps its evergreen leaves the year round. Members of this Yucca family sometimes grow 25 to 30 feet high in the warmer climates, but in the colder areas, the maximum height usually ranges between 4 to 8 feet.

This rather stately perennial has stiff evergreen, sword-like leaves which are produced in a cluster.

Yuccas are fine for bold sub-tropical effects, and because of their height, they

In northern gardens, the Yucca grows 4 to 8 ft. in height

Courtesy of The Royal Botanical Gardens, Hamilton, Ont.

Courtesy of A. B. Morse Co.

Yucca or Candle of Our Lord, keeps its evergreen leaves the year round

Laurel is a native North American shrub of compact habit which has the ability to transform bare, shady spots into places of beauty. Big clusters of flowers, varying from deep rose to pure white up to 6 inches in diameter almost completely cover the lush evergreen leathery foliage. The Mountain Laurel is thoroughly hardy and makes a well formed shrub 6 to 8 feet tall under good growing conditions. About the only

Courtesy of Sheridan Nurseries, Islington, Ont.

Yucca Filimentosa is the variety usually grown in the home garden

need planting at the back of the mixed or perennial border. They will thrive in a variety of well-drained soils, but grow best where the soil is sandy and dry. Give them a sunny location.

Filamentosa is the variety usually grown in the home garden. The attractive plants have a striking, exotic appearance, and from their centres they thrust huge spikes of creamy white, pendulant, bell-shaped flowers. You might say that these resemble huge lily-of-the-valley, and some

The evergreen Bittersweet can be easily grown as a hedge

Courtesy of Kelly Bros., Dansville, N.Y.

of them shed a heavy fragrance when open at night.

PYRACANTHA (Firethorn) — The Pyracantha is one of the most exciting and remarkable fruiting shrubs which keeps its evergreen foliage all Winter long. In the late Spring, large trusses of white flowers are produced and these are followed by an abundance of brilliant orange-scarlet berries which remain until late Winter. If you were to trace back its history, you would find it is actually a member of the rose family.

Pyracantha is an extremely good plant for the foundation planting where the soil is dry. A good location would be at the front of a house which faces south. The long vines can be trained up the side of a wall, over a doorway, or along a window casing. They are easily trimmed to fit almost any position.

Field grown or large plants of Pyracantha are difficult to transplant, so it is a good idea to buy them set in six or eight inch pots from the nursery or garden center.

Such plants will grow from 2 to 3 feet the first year. There is no vine or shrub which will produce such a quantity of eye-catching berries. The name "berry" is

The Mountain Laurel blooms in May and June

Courtesy of Sheridan Nurseries, Islington, Ont.

really incorrect as they are really small apples or pomes.

EVERGREEN BOUGHS FOR CHRISTMAS

Evergreen boughs pruned from the farm woodlot or from cull evergreens in the Christmas tree plantations can be sold to make extra money at Christmas time. Mar-keting studies conducted in New York State have confirmed this opportunity.

Red pine boughs were used in the studies but boughs from other pines or firs are also suitable. Spruce boughs are not usable because of the speed at which they shed their needles.

Boughs were sold in the form of "do-it-yourself" Christmas green kits. In addition to the boughs and twigs, each kit contained:

Firethorn (Pyracantha) a most remarkable berry bearing evergreen shrub

Courtesy of A. B. Morse Co.

Courtesy of Stark Bros. Nurseries, Louisiana, Missouri

Evergreen boughs, pine cones and apples make an attractive Christmas table center

four feet of red ribbon in the form of a bow; eight to ten pine or spruce cones (some painted silver, blue, green or red, but most left natural); eight to ten artificial red holly berries; two colored Christmas balls on pipe cleaner stems (one of which held the bow in place); a five foot coil of thin wire, a small mimeographed sheet

which listed the contents of the kit and gave some suggestions for making the decorations.

The kits were contained in attractive polyethylene bags 30 inches long, 12 inches wide and 8 inches deep. These cost about 6 cents each and had the added advantage of letting the customer see what he was

Courtesy of The Geo. J. Ball Inc., West Chicago, Ill.

Petunias out of peat pots suffer no set back when set out in the foundation planting

buying.

To prepare similar kits cones should be collected in September and October from the ground under open-grown White pine and Norway spruce. These should be brought indoors to allow them to open up in time to be ready for use in the kits in early December. A vacuum cleaner attachment can be used to spray some of the cones with red, silver, green or blue paint (enough to provide 4 colored cones for each kit). While the paint is still wet the green, red, and blue cones can be dusted with sparkling silver tinsel.

Boughs can be cut in October and November provided they are stored outside. Make sure the boughs have been cut to fit the kits before having them indoors for packing. Branches can be cut with hand pruners into appropriate-sized boughs and twigs.

The red plastic ribbon, sparkling tinsel, artificial holly berries and Christmas balls can either be obtained from a florist supply house or from a local "five and dime" store.

In selling tests, supermarkets proved to be the best outlet for these kits.

Making up these kits offers a sparetime opportunity for a family project which can provide fun as well as cash for Christmas. Such a project presents an opportunity for garden clubs, 4-H clubs or church groups to undertake a financially worthwhile activity.

Courtesy of Bristol Nurseries Inc., Bristol, Conn.

Chrysanthemums are the leading Fall perennial